Shane Gould
olympic swimmer

BY LINDA JACOBS

S0-DLE-969

EMC CORPORATION
ST. PAUL, MINNESOTA

Library of Congress Cataloging in Publication Data

Jacobs, Linda.
   Shane Gould, Olympic swimmer.

   (Her Women who win, 3)
   SUMMARY: A biography of the fifteen-year-old Australian
swimmer who won five medals — three gold, one silver,
and one bronze — at the 1972 Olympics.
   1. Gould, Shane — Juvenile literature. [1. Gould,
Shane. 2. Swimming — Biography] I. Title.
GV838.G68J32 1974 797.2'1'0924 [B] [92] 74-2228.
ISBN 0-88436-126-8
ISBN 0-88436-127-6 (pbk.)

Published by EMC Corporation
180 East Sixth Street
St. Paul, Minnesota 55101
Printed in the United States of America
0 9 8 7 6 5 4 3 2 1

WOMEN WHO WIN

JANET LYNN ★ SUNSHINE ON ICE
OLGA KORBUT ★ TEARS AND TRIUMPH
SHANE GOULD ★ OLYMPIC SWIMMER
CHRIS EVERT ★ TENNIS PRO

Shane Gould mounted the center platform at the 1972 Olympics. Applause thundered. Loudspeakers blared the Australian National Anthem. A man slipped a ribbon around Shane's neck. A shiny disc dangled from it.

Olympic gold! The fifteen-year-old swimmer had won the 200 Individual Medley.

That was a special honor for her. Shane was famous for her freestyle swimming. But in the Medley, she had to do the butterfly, the backstroke, and the breaststroke — as well as freestyle.

Australian swimming fans especially worried about the backstroke. They knew it was Shane's weakest area. Nobody thought she would win the Medley. Nobody, that is, but Shane and her coach, Forbes Carlile. He trained her for the Medley. Shane worked on it — and she won.

The Individual Medley was Shane's most surprising win at the Olympics. But it wasn't her only medal. Before the competition ended, Shane stood on the victory platform five times. She won three gold medals, one silver, and one bronze.

Every time Shane mounted the platform, she smiled and pulled herself to her full 5' 7½". Her silver blond hair glowed against tanned skin. Her sleek figure dominated the stand. The sight of her made Australians proud of this girl from their country.

Something else made them proud, too. Shane carried a battered toy kangaroo to the platform with her. It was the mascot of the Australian swim team.

That little kangaroo had been to every Olympics since 1956. Australian stars had carried it proudly as they accepted their medals. Now it was Shane Gould's turn to carry the kangaroo. She had earned the honor through talent and years of hard work.

It all began when Shane Elizabeth Gould was born on November 23, 1956. That was also the day that the 1956 Olympics began in Melbourne, Australia. The Australian swim team made its best-ever record in that Olympics.

Maybe the day of Shane's birth pointed the way to what was to come. She showed early signs of talent. She learned to walk early and she found it easy to make her body do what she wanted it to do. She liked to move, liked to be always doing something. Her parents called her over-active. By the time she turned three, Shane had started swimming.

Her career began because of a bad accident. Shane spilled scalding tea all over herself. The doctors said that swimming would help her get well. It would help heal her skin.

Luckily, Shane had plenty of places to swim. Just before the accident her family had moved from Sydney, Australia, to the Fiji Islands. Mr. Gould worked for a big airline. They had transferred him to Nandi, Fiji.

Because the Islands are surrounded by water, Shane could swim in the ocean or in quiet ponds. She could swim all day if she wanted to. And she wanted to! Shane loved the water right away. She learned to swim as easily as she had learned to walk, and soon her body healed.

Another good thing happened, too. Swimming gave Shane something to do. It gave her a way to use her great energy. Her parents liked that. They had worried about her over-activity. They had wanted something to keep her busy. Swimming filled the bill.

While living on Fiji, young Shane learned many things from the Fiji children. Shane, at left, and her sisters Debbie and Lynnette had fun wearing grass skirts and learning Fiji dances.

As much as Shane loved the water, she found time to do other things too. The children on Fiji taught her to climb palm trees. Soon, she could shinny up a tree as well as any child on the island.

Sometimes, Shane's parents worried about tree-climbing. They especially worried when Shane started jumping out of the trees. That began when she was four. Shane would hide in a palm tree and wait for her father. When he came by she'd yell, "Catch me, Daddy." Then she'd jump ten feet into his arms.

After awhile, the Goulds stopped worrying about Shane's tricks. She never hurt herself. She could swing upside down from ropes. She could climb trees. And she could swim.

Five-year-old Shane loved to climb the tall trees on Fiji. Shinnying up big coconut trees like this one helped make Shane's arms and shoulders strong for swimming.

Neither Shane nor her parents connected tree-climbing with swimming. Later, Shane's coach credited climbing all those trees for much of Shane's swimming ability. He said that tree-climbing used the same muscles as swimming. It had strengthened Shane's arms and chest.

10

When Shane was only nine she swam in school swim meets. Even then, Shane began to break records. She was on her way to the top.

So young Shane climbed trees, and she swam. She kept active and happy on Fiji until she was nine years old. Then her father was sent back to Australia. In 1966, the family settled in the city of Brisbane.

Shane's parents wanted to make her happy in her new home. So they immediately enrolled her in organized swimming. That was one of the best decisions they ever made. Within a year, Shane was swimming in competitions. Soon she started breaking records for her age-group. Shane Elizabeth Gould was on her way to becoming the best woman swimmer in the world.

The journey wasn't an easy one. At first, Shane simply enjoyed swimming. But then she got more and more involved. She entered more competitions. Then another family move started her on the Olympic trail.

Shane and her coach, Forbes Carlile, worked together at the Ryde Swimming Center. Mr. Carlile coached Shane for many years after her family moved to Sydney, Australia.

Mr. Gould's job called him to Sydney, the capital of the state of New South Wales in Australia. Shane felt unsure at first. What would this move do to the swimming she loved? Then she found Sydney's famous Ryde Swimming Center. Most important of all, she found a new coach, Forbes Carlile.

Mr. Carlile saw a champion in Shane. She had the talent and the personality to become the tops. Personality is very important in a champion. It is almost as important as talent. A talented girl who won't work will never win gold medals.

Shane would work. She organized her time well. She stayed calm in tense situations. She had that all-important drive to win. She also had an ability to lose without being crushed.

That meant a lot to Forbes Carlile. An athlete has to keep her confidence, even when she loses. She has to pick herself up and get ready for the next competition. Shane had that kind of confidence and determination.

Forbes Carlile never worried about Shane in the personality department. But he did worry about her swimming method. Shane started out as a sprinter — a short distance swimmer. Sprinters usually kick up a huge froth when they're swimming. They use their feet almost as much as they use their arms.

Shane didn't do that. Her feet barely kicked up a fine spray. Instead of kicking six times to a stroke, she kicked only two or three times.

Mr. Carlile usually taught a two-beat kick only to his **distance** swimmers. He wasn't sure about Shane. Could a sprinter get enough speed without kicking up a storm? Mr. Carlile didn't think so. He made Shane practice and practice. He tried to get her to use her legs more. It didn't work.

Shane tried. She even practiced by hanging on to a kickboard and thinking hard about her legs. But the minute she started really swimming, she fell back into the slower kick. Finally, Mr. Carlile decided to leave Shane alone. Her fluttery, two-or-three beat kick later changed into the pure two-beat kick usually used only by the distance swimmers.

That kick made Shane different from all other sprint swimmers. It also laid the groundwork for her to move up to longer events. Before long, Shane could swim every freestyle distance, from the shortest to the longest.

She became a threat to every other swimmer at the Ryde Center. Many of them were jealous of her. Karen Moras, Mr. Carlile's star distance swimmer, was especially jealous.

Shane started beating Karen. Karen thought that Mr. Carlile was paying too much attention to Shane. The problem went from bad to worse. Karen argued with Mr. Carlile and changed to another coach at the Swimming Center. Other students started booing Shane when she would win in practice swims.

That hurt Shane. She liked people and she wanted them to like her. Her family and her coach tried to help her understand. She was the new girl in town and she was beating everybody in sight. People couldn't help being jealous.

Shane tried to understand, but it was hard. Maybe the problems even hurt her confidence and her famous energy. She wasn't doing as well as Mr. Carlile knew she could. In 1970, Shane was passed over for the Commonwealth Games. She didn't make the Australian Swim Team.

Shane thought a lot about that. She didn't like losing. She wanted to be the best swimmer she possibly could. So she got down to work.

Mr. Carlile doubled her practice schedule. Shane swam more than she ever had in her life. She forgot about problems with her fellow students. Soon, those problems faded. Even Karen Moras became Shane's friend.

In her new program, Shane needed to feel that she was among friends. She also needed all of her extra energy. Her schedule would have destroyed most other people.

14

Shane's mother says good-bye as Shane hurries off to school. Students in Australia wear special school uniforms.

During the height of her training, Shane got up at 5:15 almost every morning. She staggered out of bed and grabbed a glass of orange juice. Then she hurried off to Ryde Center. There, every morning, Shane swam three or four miles.

She got back home by 7:15 and ate a huge breakfast. Then she rushed to school. She relaxed for a few minutes after classes. Then it was off to the Center again for another three or four miles of swimming.

With a schedule like that, it isn't hard to understand why 7:30 was Shane's bedtime. She went to bed that early because she was tired that early.

Even though Shane was very busy with swimming, she found time for homework and was a good student. At home after school, Shane works on her assignments.

Shane never complained about her schedule. She worked gladly. But she also kept herself a well-balanced person. She didn't let swimming rob her of other kinds of activities.

She loved to read. It helped her relax when she was too keyed up. Shane has always been a reader and probably always will be. She read four books in the one week before she set a world's record in the 100-meter freestyle.

It may seem strange for such an athletic girl to like a quiet activity like reading. But it never seemed strange to Shane. Her parents taught her that she had a mind as well as a body. Shane learned that lesson well.

16

She not only read for fun, she made good grades. She kept an "A" average in school. Sometimes, she had to study between swims to do it. But she worked and organized her time.

She organized so well that she found time for family activities too. On weekends she did yard work and home chores with her parents and her three sisters. Sometimes the whole family would go away for a weekend's rest.

They all needed the rest. Shane needed it because of her heavy training. Her parents and sisters needed it because of all the ways they helped in that training.

Shane's older sister, Lynette, did extra home chores so Shane could practice. Her two younger sisters, Debbie and Jenny, gave up their ballet lessons. Their dancing lessons came at the same time as Shane's afternoon practice. Mrs. Gould couldn't drive everybody everywhere. So Debbie and Jenny quit dancing and started swimming at Ryde Center.

The whole family gave up evening television so Shane could get plenty of sleep. None of them minded. They knew they had a future champion in the family.

As much as the Goulds helped in Shane's swimming, they cared more about her as a person. True, they wanted to see her win. But they also wanted her to be healthy and happy.

Sometimes, Mr. and Mrs. Gould worried because Shane worked so hard on her swimming. They thought she tired herself too much. They'd tell her to get more rest.

Before rushing off to swimming practice, Shane checks with her mother on what's for dinner.

Shane wouldn't always listen. She wanted to swim too much. So, once in a while, one of her parents would sneak into Shane's bedroom and set her alarm for a later time. That way she would get more rest in spite of herself.

Shane never got angry when that happened. She knew her parents were trying to help. But she didn't like missing morning training sessions.

Shane did have other ways of breaking training though. She loved to eat rich foods, like cream cakes. Mr. Carlile wanted her on a strict diet because she gained weight easily. Most of the time, Shane watched her eating. But sometimes she couldn't turn down one of her favorite treats.

She also couldn't turn down a once-in-a-while date with her boyfriend. Shane has gone out with John Williams for two years. He's a swimmer, too, and likes swimming as much as Shane does.

The two of them liked to be together. They saw each other at practice every day, and sometimes they went sailing on the Williams' family boat.

Mr. Carlile worried because sailing tired Shane. She worked hard on the boat. The next day at practice, she wouldn't work as hard as Mr. Carlile wanted her to. At those times, Mr. Carlile ordered Shane out of the pool. He did that to all his swimmers if they needed it. He expected the best from every swimmer, every time.

Shane didn't get upset those few times when she was the swimmer ordered out of the pool. Being punished made her one of the group. It showed everybody that she wasn't a favorite.

Mr. Carlile did what had to be done. And he trusted Shane's self-discipline to keep her from going too far in breaking training. He knew that she loved swimming enough to give up lots of things for it.

Shane did give up many social activities. Often she didn't have time for anything besides swimming. But Shane didn't really mind. She knew that was the price she had to pay to become a champion.

"Breaking world records is more thrilling than going to parties and out with boys," said Shane.

So Shane gave up parties. She made herself happy with seeing John at swim practice and going sailing once in awhile. She kept close to her rigid schedule and worked hard. She was level-headed enough to know when to play and when to work.

Soon Shane's sacrifices and hard work began to pay off and Shane was on her way to becoming a great champion. At competitions Shane became a popular figure. The fans loved to cheer her on.

And Shane gave them quite a heroine to cheer for. She broke everyone else's world record. Then she began breaking her own. Many people think that Shane is the best woman swimmer of all time. She has broken more world records than anyone else.

Before she even went to the Olympics, Shane held every freestyle record in the books. She set her first world record in the 400-meter freestyle. That was on July 9, 1971. Shane was only fourteen. After that, she just kept on rolling.

A proud and happy Shane Gould talks to reporters after the big meet. She had just set the world record for the 400 meter freestyle swim.

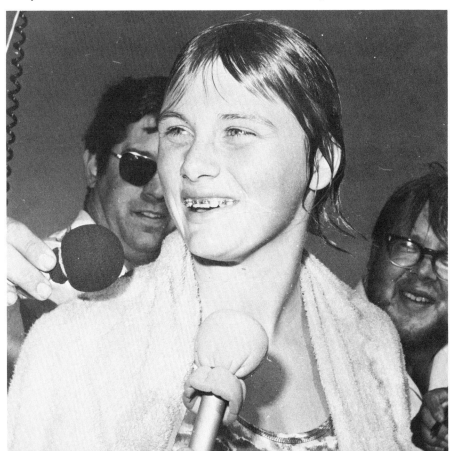

Shane pulls ahead to set a new record and win the 200 meter freestyle event.

But it wasn't always easy. Shane had to set her record for the 200-meter freestyle under the worst possible conditions.

All the swimmers had lined up on their blocks. Shane leaned forward. Her arms reached back. Her legs tensed, ready to push off. Then she lost her balance. Just at that minute, the starting gun cracked. Shane struggled for balance. Everyone else hit the water before she did.

The referee tried to stop the race. But the rope he had to pull to close off the lanes wouldn't move. It was stuck. He had no choice but to let the race go on.

Shane knew she had a lot of making up to do. She pushed herself. She used all her famous energy and her skill. She quickly caught up to the other swimmers. Then she passed them. She kept driving, kept pushing. When the race was over, Shane had won. She had also set a new world record.

Shane's training and determination helped her give that great performance. Her usual attitude before a race also helped her.

In the locker rooms, most swimmers chatter and laugh. They try to relax by having a good time. Shane never did that. She would find a corner to herself. She wouldn't speak to anyone before a race.

If someone tried to start a conversation, she ignored them. Strangers didn't understand this. They thought Shane was snubbing them. Shane didn't want to hurt anyone's feelings, but she had to have her quiet time.

Her friends and family did understand. They stayed out of her way before a race. But it took awhile for her boyfriend to learn about that part of Shane's personality.

At first, John got hurt because she ignored him, and Shane got mad because John bothered her. Finally, they had a fight. Then John learned that Shane didn't mean to hurt him. It was her way of preparing for a race. Once he understood, he simply let her alone. Once again, Shane had her time to get mentally ready for the coming race.

That mental readiness helped her get the extra burst she needed to come from behind and break the 200-meter record. It also helped her when she broke the 100-meter freestyle record.

An Australian swimmer named Dawn Fraser set that record in 1964. Shane tied the 58.9-second time at a meet in London, England. But she wanted to break the record. She didn't want to share it with anybody. That meant she had to swim the 100-meter race in 58.8 seconds — tops.

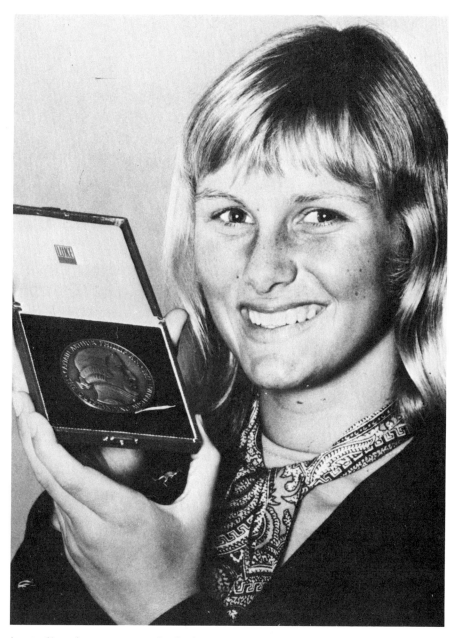

Australian fans are proud of Shane Gould, the Olympic champion. After her great showing at the 1972 Olympics, she was presented with the Australian of the Year award for 1972.

Could she do it? She planned to try at the New South Wales meet on January 17, 1972. All of Australia rooted for her. Radio and TV announcers talked about the coming race. Newspaper headlines declared, "Shane Seeks Impossible Feat." Excitement gripped the country.

The excitement was high in the Gould household too. Mr. Gould hung a sign on Shane's bedroom door. It read, "The 588 Club." That showed the 58.8 time Shane needed to make in order to break the tie.

Shane hoped she could do it! This was the most important record of all. She once called the 100-meter event, "the one with all the ribbons around it." She wanted it more than she'd wanted anything else in her swimming career.

On the day of the race, Shane withdrew more than usual. She went into a world of her own. She hardly noticed the thousands of people crowding the pool. Even the excitement of a nationwide TV hookup didn't move her.

One thing did bother her. The TV network asked race officials to move up the 100-meter event by half an hour. The officials agreed. They told all the swimmers — all but Shane.

Somehow, Shane never got word. A minute before the new race time, an official told her to get to the starting block. Shane started to cry. Why hadn't anyone told her? She later said it was like expecting a cold engine to start without a warm-up time.

She had her cry. Then she went to the starting block. There were no more tears. Shane stood ready. The starting gun cracked. She dove for water.

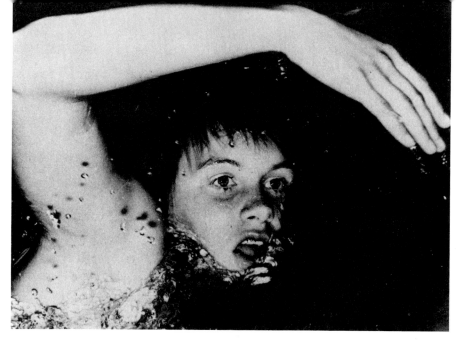

Shane in action. The star shows the swimming form which made her a champion.

Exactly 58.5 seconds later she had won. And she had lopped off almost half a second from the old record. People cheered. Shane grinned. The next day's newspapers blared the headline, "Shane Does It Again!"

Shane went on to win a total of eight events in the New South Wales meet. She was proud of her performance. But a strange thing began to happen. The audience that had cheered her world records gave only polite applause to her other wins.

People expected a record to crack every time Shane dove into the water. She didn't break records in her other seven wins. So the cheering wasn't as loud.

Newspapers also thought that Shane should always break records. When she won the 100-meter butterfly, headlines didn't say that. They said, "Shane Gould Fails to Set Record in 100 Butterfly."

25

Back home in Australia after the 1972 Olympics, Shane proudly shows off her five Olympic medals.

That public attitude put Shane to a great personal test as she went into the Olympics. Australians expected her to bring home barrels of gold medals. They expected nothing less than perfection from the famous Miss Gould.

Shane wanted to please the Australian people — and herself. She wanted her coach to be proud of her. She wanted her family to feel that all their sacrifices for her swimming had been worth it.

Shane was only fifteen years old at that time. How could such a young girl stand all that pressure? Somehow, Shane did stand it. Her self-confidence helped. Her ability to draw into herself helped. And Shane's family helped her.

Perhaps in those trying days before the Olympics Shane remembered a telegram her parents had once sent her. The telegram came when she tied the 100-meter record at a meet in London. "Remember, it is your modesty and your talent which have made you great," said the telegram from Shane's parents.

Shane may not have remembered those exact words before the Olympics. But she lived the basic message. She kept a quiet faith in herself. She kept her balance and her determination to win. And win she did, ending up with three gold medals, one silver, and one bronze for first place, second place, and third place.

26

Olympic contestants arrived early in Munich to get in some last minute practice time. At the Munich Olympic pool Shane worked on her time and strokes before the big events.

The practice paid off. Shane won the gold medal at Munich for the 200 meter individual medley and again set a new world record.

As the Olympics continued, Shane kept on winning. Here she churns through the water, pushing to win the 400 meter freestyle event.

Exhausted, but victorious, Shane climbs out of the Olympic pool after winning her second Olympic gold medal in the 400 meter freestyle.

Olympic winners Shane Gould and Mark Spitz share the spotlight at the 1972 Olympics.

Her five medals in the 1972 Munich Olympics are now history. At only fifteen, Shane became internationally famous. She was on top. But where does a young girl go from the top?

After some time, Shane started getting tired of swimming. She wasn't sure she wanted to continue. She wasn't sure she could keep herself in the proper frame of mind.

There were no new worlds to conquer. Shane could only do what she had already done. True, at the next Olympics she might win more medals. But the next Olympic games were four years away. Shane would be nineteen. That seemed a long time away.

Finally, Shane decided to quit swimming. Mr. Carlile tried to talk her out of it. He said that a trip to the United States might perk her up. It might give her those new worlds to conquer. Shane's parents agreed.

Proudly wearing her Olympic blazer, the young Australian heroine returns home to rest and relax. Shane was the youngest Australian athlete ever to win an Olympic gold medal.

So Shane went to the United States for five months. She won some races and she lost some. When she won, people acted like that was the normal thing for Shane Gould to be doing. When she lost, they acted shocked.

In the United States Shane still followed a busy training schedule. Towel in hand, she heads to the pool for a practice session after a full day at school in California.

32

The Olympic-sized pool at Foothill College became Shane's practice center in California. If she was to go on to the 1976 Olympics, she would have to swim 4000 miles in three years. It was getting to be a tough schedule.

School work still had to be done, too. Between practice sessions and traveling to meets, Shane tried to find the time to keep up with her studies.

Shane kept working. And she kept winning. In the International meet in London in 1973, Shane won three individual events. But after five months in California, Shane decided to go home.

Back in Australia, Shane returned to practice at the Ryde Swimming Center and to her coach, Mr. Forbes Carlile.

36

Even though she had a busy schedule of her own, Shane found time to do some coaching herself by helping younger swimmers at the Ryde Center.

Shane didn't find her new world in America. She went back to Australia, discouraged and 24 pounds overweight. She told Mr. Carlile and her family that she definitely wanted to quit swimming.

Again, Mr. Carlile tried to change Shane's mind. Something happened that he thought might make Shane want to keep going. An East German girl named Kornelia Ender broke Shane's prized 100-meter record. Kornelia swam the 100-meter in 58.25. That was one-fourth of a second better than Shane's time. Coach Carlile hoped Shane would want to recapture the record. He hoped she would work harder than ever.

Swimming fans started talking about the coming battle of champions between Shane and Kornelia. They said it would begin at the World Swimming Championships. Many thought it would carry on into the 1976 Olympics.

Everyone got excited at the idea of that battle. But it will never happen. Shane stuck to her decision. She wouldn't change her mind. She was tired and she felt she had fame enough to last a lifetime. In July of 1973, Shane Gould announced her retirement from swimming. A great athletic career had ended.

Australians protested that Shane was their greatest hope for the 1976 Olympics. How could she leave the team? What would they do without her?

Shane drew into herself much the way she always had before her races. The whole Gould family thought that Shane had done enough in swimming. It was time for her to think of other things. But what other things?

After all those years of swimming, Shane had to find a whole new direction. She didn't know what she wanted to do. She had to find another life to replace the one she had already lived.

Shane may be uncertain as she faces that task. Like all teenagers, she will have to question herself. She will search for her place in life. And she will surely find it. A girl who can go from climbing palm trees to breaking world records has everything on her side.

ACKNOWLEDGMENTS

PHOTO CREDITS

Australian Information Service, 12, 15, 18, 23, 37; Gould, Shane, 9, 10, 11, 34; Swimming World Photo, cover (Margie Shuer), 16, 31, 39 (Tony Duffy); United Press International, 7, 20, 27, 28 (bottom), 32, 33 (top); Wide World Photos, 21, 25, 28 (top), 29, 31, 33 (bottom), 35, 36.

The author and publisher express special thanks to Shane Gould and her family for their invaluable assistance in making this book possible.